INTRODUCTION

The Jumping Jack is a very old toy which has been part of the culture of many countries throughout the world. Probably in no place, however, has it enjoyed the popularity it has in France where in the eighteenth century the Jumping Jack or *pantin* became not only a plaything for children but an amusement for adults. During this period members of the French court competed with each other for the largest collection, and famous artists began to design Jumping Jacks.

This collection of 11 antique French Jumping Jacks was published by Pellerin, one of the most celebrated firms of printers in the small French city of Epinal. The city of Epinal in the Vosges mountains of Lorraine is synonymous the world over with colorful and popular prints *(imagerie)*, and the paper toys and paper dolls produced there are world renowned. (See Epinal: *Antique Paper Dolls: The Edwardian Era,* Dover 0-486-23175-5.)

Many of the antique Jumping Jacks which appear in this collection are modeled after the traditional characters in the Commedia dell' Arte, the name given to the Renaissance and Baroque Italian theatrical genre in which the plot is written out, but the dialogue is improvised by the actors. Certain principal characters, such as Harlequin, Polichinelle, Pierrette, Pierrot and Columbine who are represented in this collection, appear in virtually all plays of this type. Once you have cut out and strung these Jumping Jacks, you can perform your own traditional comedies or simply enjoy these Jumping Jacks as toys, party favors or hang them as decorations.

The following materials will be necessary to make your Jumping Jacks:

Sharp scissors or X-Acto knife: for cutting out the parts of the Jumping Jacks.

Heavy thread, thin string or crochet cotton: for stringing the figures.

Large needle: for making holes and stringing the figures.

Small brass paper fasteners (available in variety and stationery shops): for holding the sections of each figure together.

Since these antique Jumping Jacks were intended to be made up by people who understood how they were to be put together, very little printed instruction appears on most of the toys. Unless you are very experienced with making Jumping Jacks it is probably best to start with either the Harlequin on Plate 1 or the Pierrot on Plate 2, as these toys have numbered holes. The instructions printed below refer specifically to these two toys. Once you have strung either the Harlequin or the Pierrot, you can follow the same procedure for making the other toys which have no numbers printed on them.

Carefully cut out the parts. With your needle make a hole in the center of each circle (which indicates where the paper fasteners are to be placed). Make another hole for the strings in the arms and upper legs $\frac{1}{8}''$ to $\frac{3}{16}''$ away from holes 1, 2, 3 and 4.

Following the diagram below, line up the parts of your Harlequin or Pierrot, matching the numbers, and insert a brass paper fastener in each hole. Attach the two sections of each leg first, then attach the legs and the arms to the body. The fasteners must be secured loosely enough to allow for easy movement of the parts. In order to achieve this you may find it helpful to use a special cardboard spacer which you can make yourself. Trace the pattern given below for the spacer and cut one from a piece of corrugated cardboard.

Insert the paper fasteners and twist them around in the holes until the fasteners can move easily. Then insert the cardboard spacer between the two parts of each fastener so that the spacer slot fits snugly around the fastener. Spread out the prongs of the fastener and remove the spacer. Move the parts around again to make sure that they move easily. Remember to use the spacer every time you use a brass fastener.

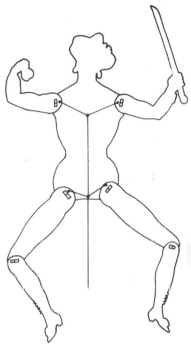

Once the parts are attached, the figure is ready to be strung. Refer again to the diagram showing the Harlequin from the rear. To string the Harlequin, hold the figure so that the arms are hanging straight down behind the body. Push a threaded needle into the hole at the top of one of the arms. Knot the string several times so that it is attached securely. Bring the string across the back and attach it to the other arm. Tie the string so that it is taut when the arms hang down. Cut off the excess string. In the same manner attach the two legs with another short string. Next, with the arms and legs hanging straight down and the strings taut, attach a new piece of string at the center of the first string between the two arms and then to the string between the legs. This third string is the control string. When you pull down on the control string, the arms and legs should move upward. When you let the string go, the parts should fall back easily.

If the control string does not work correctly, try stringing the figure again. Stringing the Jumping Jack is actually very simple once you have tried it a few times and understand how the strings work.

When you are satisfied with your Jumping Jack, you may want to make a hole in the top of the toy and attach a string which will allow you to hang the figure.

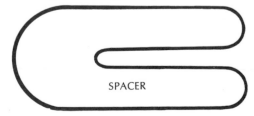

SPACER

Plate 1
HARLEQUIN

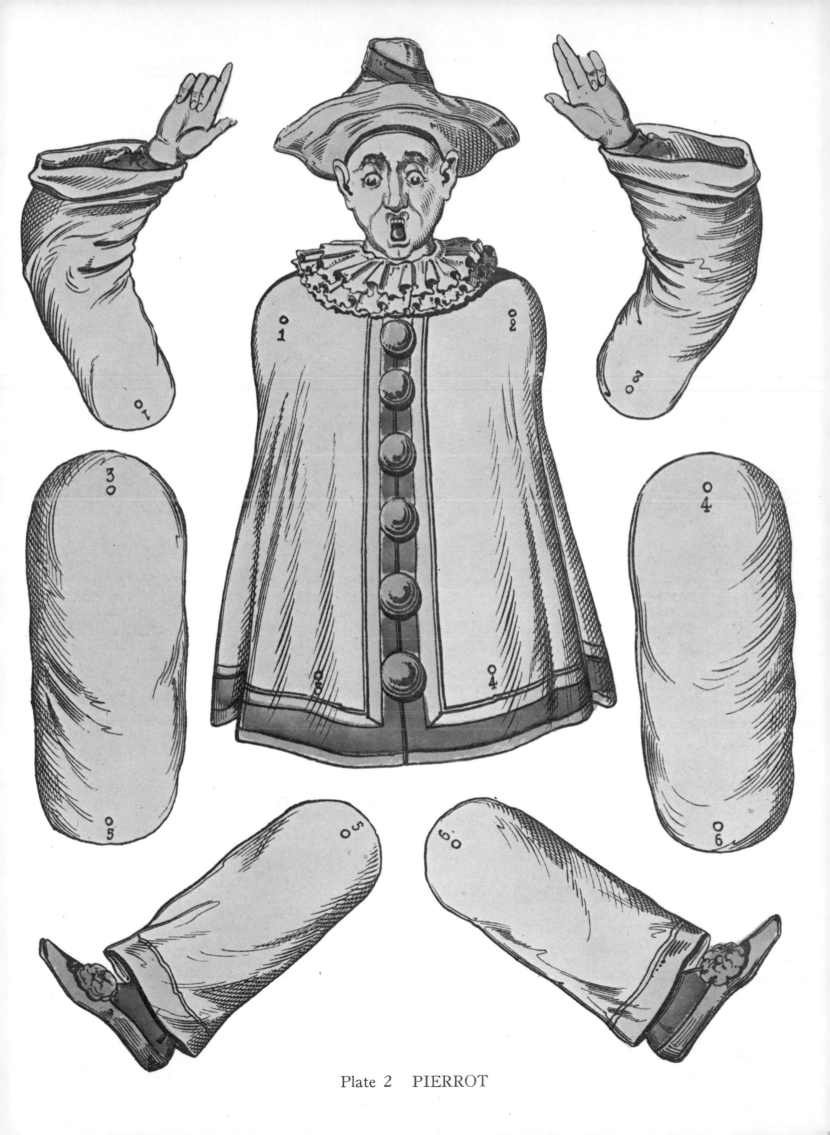

Plate 2   PIERROT

Plate 3 POLICHINELLE

Plate 4 COLUMBINE

Plate 5   HARLEQUIN

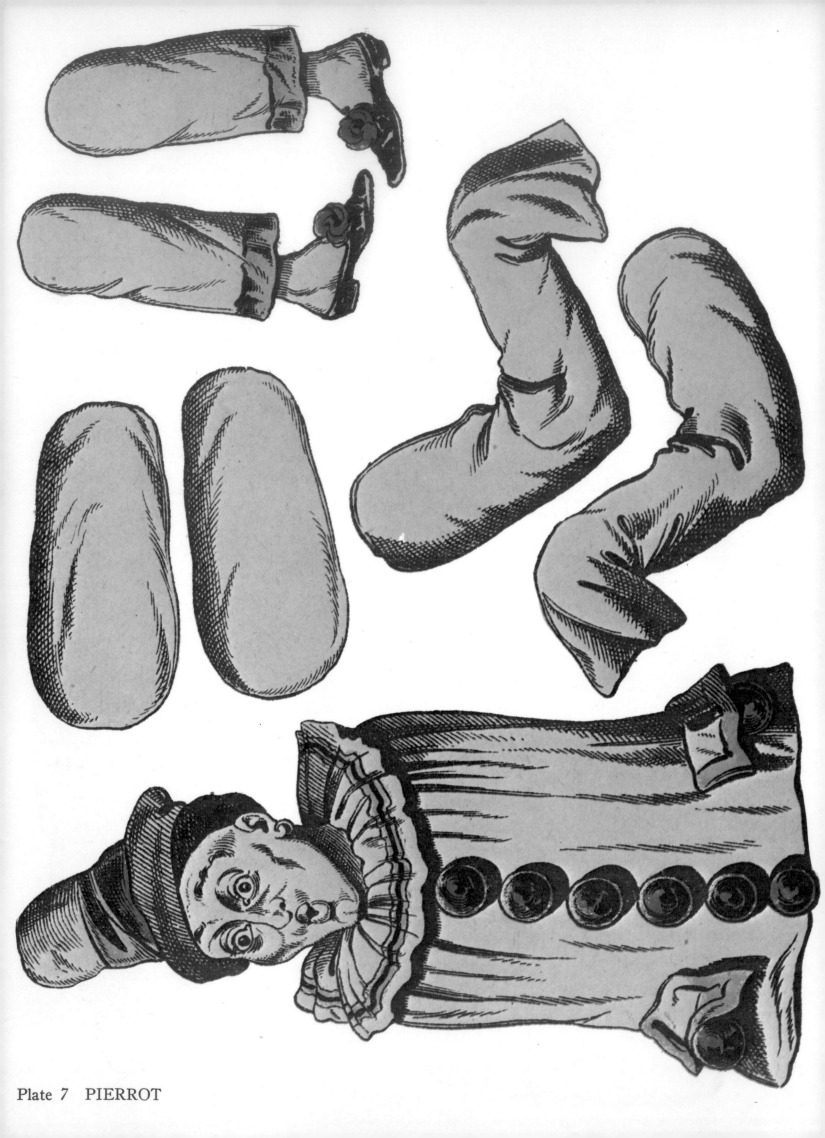

Plate 7   PIERROT

Plate 8 PIERRETTE

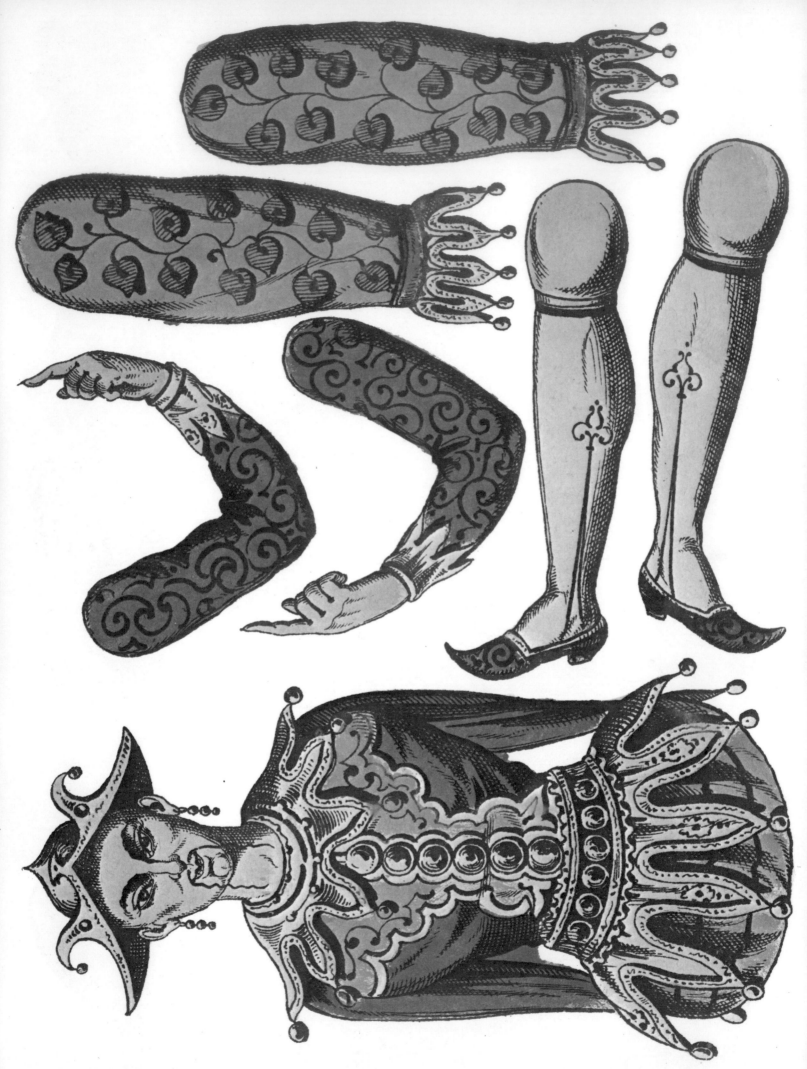

Plate 9 CHINESE DANCER

Plate 10   CHINESE DANCER

Plate 11 PIERRETTE